Beyond Sex: Towards an Unfettered Intimacy

⊗≫⊗

Copyright © 2021 Felix Bamirin

Other books by Felix Bamirin: *Mastering Negative Emotions, Marriage on a Mission, Forgiving Forward, Ultimate Treasure, A Parent's Guide to Raising a Happy & Confident Child*

Cover Photo by: Vicadexprints
Editor: Sherilynn Asuoha | 7th Seal Advantage

Printed in the United States of America
First Printing Edition, 2021

ISBN 978-1-7367315-0-5

~*Esther Adenike Bamirin*~

Behold, thou art fair, my love.

Behold, thou art fair;

Thou hast doves' eyes within thy locks: thy hair is as a flock

of goats, that appear from mount Gilead.

Thy teeth are like a flock of sheep that are even shorn,

which came up from the washing; whereof everyone bear

twins, and none is barren among them.

Thy lips are like a thread of scarlet, and thy speech is

comely: thy temples are like a piece of a pomegranate

within thy locks.

Thy two breasts are like two young roes that are twins,

which feed among the lilies.

Until the daybreak, and the shadows flee away,

I will get me to the mountain of myrrh, and to the hill of

frankincense.

Thou art all fair, my love; there is no spot in thee".

-*Song of Solomon 4:1-7, KJV-*

CONTENTS

Introduction: Beyond Sex   1

1   Sex Power   5

2   Naked + Unashamed   22

3   Secret Pleasures   33

4   Secret Treasures   45

5   Sexpectations   52

6   Fantasy   62

7   Closer + Deeper   69

8   Case Studies   87

Conclusion   93

Acknowledgements   98

INTRO

BEYOND SEX

Before we get started, let me caution you that this book is written specifically for married couples who have chosen to follow Christ. Maybe it can be for Christians preparing for marriage, but mainly, it is for those of us who are married. Why? I want to address the attitudes of Christian couples towards sexual intimacy.

If you do not fit into both of these categories, this book might not make sense to you and the benefits definitely will not work for you. If you are married or engaged to be married and you have not yet chosen to follow Christ and you desire to make that choice, I would love to give you the opportunity so that you can get the most out of this book and so that I see you on the other side of eternity. Simply say aloud:

Lord Jesus, I acknowledge I am a sinner, and I believe You have the power to save me. I believe You were crucified on the cross for my sins and that you died, were buried and rose again with all power and are seated at the right hand of the Father. I believe you are returning. I declare that You, alone are my Lord and Savior. I choose to follow you. Thank You, Heavenly Father, in Jesus' mighty name I pray.

If you prayed this prayer, congratulations and welcome to the family of God! Your next step is to get rooted in a godly church.

Now that we have settled the critical requirement of both marriage and salvation as it pertains to the pages in this book, let's talk about sex. How can we enhance and maximize the blessing of sex in our marriages? With all the boundaries in place around sex, is there even room for enhancement? Yes, there are very clear dos and don'ts of sexual intercourse. We will discuss those later. More importantly, there are major benefits in enjoying a healthy sex life that we must also address so that we don't miss out on or ignore any of the gifts and advantages God has made available for us on this side of eternity.

Good sex is key to keeping infidelity, marital frustration, crisis, separation and divorce rates low among believers. In this book is practical, biblical help on how to set behaviors and patterns that will make sexual connections easier between couples. As you read, you will develop a deeper understanding of the sexual nature of the sexes.

By the end of this book, I pray you and your spouse will have increased your physical touch, communication and overall intimacy. When this happens, you will see that you begin to experience a deeper spiritual connection as well.

You will notice that you are truly becoming one flesh by how effortlessly you become and remain aligned with each other and with the Holy Spirit (Don't worry we will shed more light on this later).

I encourage you to read and study this book with your spouse. Take time to digest it together and pray together… and lay together. Be blessed as you read.

1

SEX POWER

Then God blessed them, and God said to them, "Be fruitful and multiply; fill the earth and subdue it; have dominion…
Genesis 1:28

Sex is powerful, but the culture of today teaches us to regard it as common. Nowadays, everything is sexy, isn't it? Sex that was originally designed and understood as sacred and intimate has become commercialized at best. At its worst, it is in its deviant form and criminalized. Our world has become so grossly sexualized, that for many, the very idea of this beautiful spiritual stimulant and enhancer is now numbing and dissociating.

After worship, sex is the most powerful, productive force of engagement between two living beings God ever created. Just like worship, sex is a powerful and productive force of engagement between two living beings that God created. Sex is life- giving just as worship and koinonia with God in Christ is life-giving. As we share a deep bond with the Lord in worship, so also is the union between a man and his wife, a deep bond capable of creating unspeakable manifestations in the earth.

The devil knows this and as he does with all sacred things, he hijacked and perverted it until it became common knowledge that "sex sells" and lesser known that "sex seals"[1].

THE TRUE POWER OF SEX

These days cars, clothes and the like are measured with the same sex appeal God ascribed to the men He breathed His Spirit into. Sex is known in the context of

---

[1] According to 1 Corinthians 6:16

prostitution or sex work- a business, one of the oldest occupations in the world. It is so commercialized that as we speak, people around the world are fighting for the right to buy and sell sex freely and without penalty (or so they think).

Sex is known in the context of violence, with local and federal arms of law enforcement dedicated to addressing sex crimes and human trafficking. People know that sex has power but only in the lowest of contexts. People know it is powerful enough to be used as a political statement- an opportunity to rebel or gain control when issues of identity and belonging arise.

But many people do not understand the true power of sex, especially those who should be most empowered to use it for their advantage- married, Christian couples. That is why I am writing this book.

The power of sex seems to be known in every way except as a power source. Before I explain sex power, let's take a moment to reflect on the definition of power.

POWER SUPPLY

The word power is both a noun and a verb. In either event, power supplies the opportunity and capacity for something to take place in a particular way. It is a supplier, director and an influencer. Power can change a course of events. Power is a mover and a disrupter of current events or statuses. Power also means to "move or travel with a great deal of force" (Oxford, 2021)[2].

When I talk about sex power, I am talking about the unique forces of sex that hold the audacity to change things for you and your spouse. Sex has the capacity to supply, direct, and influence you and your lover. Sex expedites processes for you, and it can change atmospheres for you. Sex expedites processes for you. Every working marital relationship understands that differences are resolved more

---

[2] All definitions are an abridged summary of Oxford Language and Google Dictionary retrieved January 2021 from https://languages.oup.com/google-dictionary-en/.

quickly in bed than on conference tables. Sex allows emotional and physical tensions to dissolve more quickly. Attention to other matters are smoother when the matter of sex is fully addressed and attended to.

The next time you have sex with your husband or wife, have this in mind and trust that your sexual experience will climax to new levels.

SEALING POWER

Sex carries an officiating power. Think about the first kiss you took with your spouse after you were pronounced husband and wife. That kiss is not only the prelude to sex, but also the announcement that your joining is official. It seals the deal.

Shortly after the ceremony comes the honeymoon and your first marriage bed encounter. It is at this time that the most intimate parts of you and your spouse lock, physically and spiritually, forming a seal that declares what

God has joined together, no man should dare to try and separate[3].

THE POWER OF ONENESS

We talk about the power of sex as a sealant. But what is it sealing? When your bodies come together as husband and wife, the act itself is a reflection of the oneness God has called you to. Paul said in his letter to the Romans:

> *For I am persuaded that neither death, nor life, nor angels, nor principalities, nor powers, nor things present, nor things to come, nor height, nor depth, nor any other creature, shall be able to separate us from the love of God, which is in Christ Jesus our Lord.*
> ### *Romans 8:8-9*

Good sex is attuned sex. That is why your mind should not be elsewhere. You should be fully in tune with your spouse's needs, desires and likes.

Do you remember radios and how you had to tune the knob or needle to just the right frequency in order to hear

---

[3] Mark 10:9

your desired radio station? The same goes for intimacy between married couples. In order to give and receive the best sexual experience for your spouse, both of your needles must be tuned in to just the right frequency. Frequency in this regard promotes oneness. But frequency with regard to intervals and your routines and consistency in having sexual intercourse with your spouse is important as well.

FREQUENCY

Sex is not for physical pleasure alone (though it is a much-appreciated bonus, don't you agree?). Sex is an opportunity to build that habit of alignment or oneness. Make your union stronger by having sex as frequently as possible because it strengthens your marital bond. Having frequent sexual intercourse with your spouse reduces tensions and other opportunities for Satan to try to tear you apart. It increases your oneness and reduces the challenges that your differences often bring into your marriage.

To achieve oneness is to achieve one of God's original intentions for marriage. It is in that unity and oneness that your marriage can glorify God. Trying marriage with any intent other than oneness will be tiresome, if not deadly to you, your spouse, and your destinies. If you cannot establish oneness in marriage, rest assured, you will have problems walking in oneness with Jesus.

THE POWER OF PRODUCTIVITY

In the book of Genesis, the first instruction God gives mankind is to "be fruitful and to multiply". He tells them to "fill the earth and subdue it"[4]. To subdue something is to get the better of it. When you subdue something, you control and overwhelm it, not the other way around[5]. Sometimes, we let the world get the best of us. We find it difficult to subdue things we actually have authority to control. The heavy

---

[4] Genesis 1:28-29
[5] Oxford Language Dictionary

amounts of stress, the distractions of life and everything else we have been unable to subdue push us into anxiety and make productivity difficult.

Life can get very busy, don't you agree? When life gets so busy for married couples, their first inclination is to believe they do not have time for sex. That is dangerous! When life gets busy, you and your spouse must get busier with each other if you know what I mean. You might even want to increase the spontaneity and frequency of sex during such times as much as possible.

Pay close attention to the times when life seems to take the most out of you: after fulfilling a major task, after exhaustive preaching tours (for people like me) or any time you have just operated heavily under the anointing, generally. When these things take place, it is important that you take notice and take precaution.

Failure to be in tune with your needs or the needs of your spouse can open the door for lust and other vulnerabilities that could be easily subdued with something as simple as a planned date night with dinner out and some passionate sex between husband and wife immediately after a taxing event.

Sex is a pacifier. It is designed to help you subdue stress and other unwanted feelings of overwhelm. For married couples who have ever tried to conceive, will you agree with me that your chances of producing a baby are far higher when you are not under pressure?

In Genesis, God was comfortable charging man with the weight of the world because He put everything in place to make it possible, including the institution of marriage and sexual intercourse. When you are relaxed and fully aware of the pacifying, peace-producing agents of sex, you are in a much better position to be productive in every sense of the word.

POWER OF AGREEMENT

Sex is your power of agreement. Jesus emphasized the power of agreement as oneness and singleness of purpose. He says, "If the two of you shall agree as touching anything on earth, it shall be done to them". Like the tower of Babel, nothing shall be impossible for the people if they were speaking one language.

Again, one will chase a thousand and two will chase, not two thousand but ten thousand. That is the power of agreement in any relationship. In marriage, agreement is strengthened on the marriage bed. Sex, through the power of spousal agreement gives power and strength to your marriage and puts the family in a better position to achieve whatsoever they set their hearts to do under God.

Whatever makes you one, united and agreeable in Christ Jesus, you must emphasize and do more often. Sex in marriage is definitely one of those things and you should maximize its potential to make your marriage stronger in resisting temptations and standing in God's purpose for your lives.

THE POWER OF OPPORTUNITY

Sex gives you an opportunity to choose to please the Lord. In the world of options that we live in, where you can choose to have sex with multiple partners and engage in all sorts of sexual immoralities, your choice to keep it within your covenant as husband and wife is an act of uncommon obedience to God and God is so pleased with you for that.

Lot remained righteous before God as long as his soul was grieved by the harmful sexual practices of those around him and as long as he remained committed to the pattern and ordinance of God regarding sexual relations which states that must be between a husband and a wife. He did not succumb to the prevailing homosexual behaviors around him. He did not only remain faithful to his wife, but it bothered his soul as an intercessor over the practices of the people among whom he lived.

God is glorified when the believer takes the opportunity to make such a powerful, yet unpopular decision to stay with God no matter what everyone else celebrates around them. God is pleased and glorified when you are willing to obey Him though there are forbidden fruits at the very center of the garden of our lives.

As an unmarried person, you glorify God by abstaining from sex with a desire to be involved only with the person to whom you will be married legally, traditionally or whatever constitutes marriage in your custom. Your viewing sex as sacred and obeying God is your power gained from purity that is aimed at not just being a proud virgin but aimed ultimately at living in obedience to and love for God.

THE POWER OF PURITY

There is a spiritual power that comes through the obedience of faith and the power of purity. The agreement to abstain from sex even in marriage for fasting purpose between husband and wife is a powerful force. It is also the understanding of how to use your sex power to achieve God's greatest glory and honor.

You do not allow yourself to be brought under the power of anything. There are times God will need your perfect attention without the distraction of any attachment to anything including your spouse. You must be willing to communicate that effectively to your spouse.

As Paul warned, I will also warn, let it be for a really limited time. God will always be there whenever you want to devote yourself to Him unto eternity, but your spouse will not always be there for all eternity. Sorry, there is no marriage in heaven. However, we will be too engrossed with the beauty of God, of Christ and of our assignment and identity in heaven that we won't even miss being married.

It does not yet appear what we shall be, but when He appears, we will see him as he is.
1 John 3:1-2

MORE THAN PHYSICAL

Sexual intercourse is more than a sensational activity. It is a deeply spiritual act of worship done in honor of God who instituted marriage and with honor to your spouse. Marital sex achieves the grand purpose of redemption. What is the grand purpose of redemption? It is perfect harmony between man and His creator.

The union between man and woman as husband and wife was created to reflect the relationship Christ Jesus desires to have with all mankind as His church. When Jesus gave us His Holy Spirit, it was so that a deeper sense of intimacy would be possible. We can have the mind and heart of Christ just by being fully consumed by His Spirit.

SEX UNITES HUSBAND AND WIFE

Remember, we discussed the act of sex as one of the processes by which oneness in marriage is achieved more than any other thing. It is a process by which a husband and wife share their lives and the substance of their bodies with each other under God in the deepest intimate way.

This uniting power of sex is not just physical, it has spiritual implications. Let's look at this Bible verse:

Know ye not that he which is joined to a harlot is one body? For two, saith he, shall become one flesh.
1 Corinthians 6:16

Sex is powerful enough to spiritually chain you to anyone you have ever had sex with. If this happens, it means you will carry all the negative issues of your exes including demonic substances and many other negative spiritual presences that may be present in their bloodlines.

Many have been infected with more spiritually transmitted infections through their past sexual partners than physical sexually transmitted diseases. This opens their souls and family lines to demons.

It is my prayer that you will recognize the true power of sex and why it must be preserved for marriage alone and mastered in the sanctity of holy matrimony.

2

NAKED +
UNASHAMED

*...And they were both naked, the man and his wife,
and were not ashamed.*
Genesis *2:25*

My wife and I have a family and marriage ministry called Family Eden. We call it such because there is so much to learn about healthy family dynamics from the set-up of Eden based on what we read in the Bible. Eden was paradise.

Eden was an atmosphere that maintained everything the first family needed to enjoy life to the fullest, especially freedom. They were free in the presence of God. They were free in front of one another, naked, and unashamed.

PARADISE

Let's talk for a minute about what made Eden a paradise and how we can apply these characteristics to our sex lives.

HABITUAL SATISFACTION

You are created to be a place of habitual satisfaction for your spouse. They are created to be the same for you. As indicated in the first few chapters of Genesis, Eden was a place of presence and provision. They had everything they needed, and in abundance.

Adam and Eve had plenty in the garden. They had everything in the presence of God. They had exactly what they needed in each other. It was good… and it was enough. Anything that did not look good to God, anything that did not seem to be good for Adam, God addressed[6]. This is the attitude we should take to communicating our sexual needs and desires to pleasure our spouse.

Can your spouse find everything they need in you? Do you spend enough time studying them to know that they might be in need of something? God in you grants you the capacity to satisfy your spouse in exceeding abundance.

Take on the mindset of withholding nothing from your spouse. Take on a mindset of excellent provision and availability to them, spiritually, mentally and physically. Your spouse can experience that state of habitual satisfaction from you just as all of your sexual needs can be met in them.

---

[6] "It is not good for man to be alone; I will make him a helper comparable to Him," Genesis 2:18

EXPLORING AND NAMING

In Eden, Adam and Eve could explore and ask questions without shame. They explored and learned things together. The only two times they were made to feel less than confident about their curiosity or discoveries was when Satan appeared as a serpent to make them second guess what they understood as truth and when they were finally exposed to sin and for the first time, they saw themselves as missing something and were ashamed.

Before the shame, one thing that made Eden to be paradise was the enjoyment of exploration. They walked through the garden, together. They learned about all God had made available to them, together. They were safe, secure and satisfied with each other in the presence and will of God. When they learned about new things, God gave them authority to name them. Tell me, when is the last time you and your spouse did some exploring? When last could your spouse tell you something they noticed and admired about your body and desired to try out? Did you explore it together and name it with them?

As we read in Genesis 2:25, Adam and Eve were in the Garden of Eden, naked and unashamed. They were naked in knowledge, in spirit and physically, yet they felt safe and secure, and satisfied. Sex is action, yes, but it should also be a place of your total presence and it should leave you both feeling safe, secure and satisfied.

When you are curious, when you are burning with desire…when you want to know how something feels, can you ask your spouse? Can you reveal your deepest sexual desires and urges to them and know that when you do, you'll be safe, your marriage will be secure, and you will be satisfied with your partner's response? Can your spouse do the same with you freely, without guilt or shame?

Take a moment to ask each other these questions. Talk about why you can or cannot safely share your most intimate questions or desires and truths with your spouse.

The degree to which you can be naked before one another should be exponentially greater than any degree of shame you experience. The first challenge I am going to give you is that you make it a goal to be habitually naked physically, emotionally and spiritually before your spouse. Make it easy for them to do the same with you.

NAKED

To be naked is to be transparent and honest. You can't hide any part of you in nakedness. And when it comes to your relationship with your spouse, that is the reflection of the relationship between Christ and His church, nothing should be hidden. Nothing should be off limits. The love should be unconditional, and we should be fully submitted.

BE VULNERABLE

Nakedness is a state of vulnerability. It leaves you completely exposed, accessible and open for judgement, contact and impact. Vulnerability is a challenge for many of us. Why? It's mostly hard because we have become vulnerable with the wrong people and about the wrong things in the past and this has caused us some form of pain, shame or embarrassment, much like Adam and Eve's experience with the serpent. The serpent was allowed to weigh in on what was between Adam, Eve and their God.

Vulnerability is not bad. It is not a sign of weakness. In fact, it is a sign of great strength and maturity- that is if you are vulnerable with the right person at the right time and in the right context. Vulnerability is necessary for one to become whole and for two whole people to become one with his or her spouse- this is a foundational principle for a fruitful marriage. Vulnerability allows the right person to see where you need healing or fulfillment and give you what you need.

UNASHAMED

The ability to be naked and unashamed are indicative of the level of intimacy you have with your spouse. The more intimate you are, the less you have to hide. A clear sign that Adam and Eve were no longer in alignment with God, their father, was that they were ashamed.

They were more concerned about how they might be perceived than they were about their breached covenant with God at that time. They were more focused on hiding their innermost thoughts than getting help or repairing the relationship and trust that had been breached with each other (by blaming one another) and with the Holy Spirit.

TRUST

Adam and Eve were already naked and had been since their conception. Why were they suddenly ashamed? There was a lack of trust and not because God had proven Himself untrustworthy. God had not threatened them or ever made them feel unsafe. It was all in their minds. They had betrayed each other's trust by blaming one another. And now, they had the idea that God, too, could devalue them as they had done each other.

Once they had the consequence of how they made each other feel, for the first time ever, they learned what it was like not to feel good. Perhaps they were afraid that the God they knew as good would respond in a way that felt as bad as they did in the moment, which didn't feel very safe or secure at the time.

Trust is key in relationship. Trust God. Be sure that God can trust you with the spouse He has given you. Trust your spouse and show your spouse that he or she can trust you. The benefits of being naked and unashamed are that you can get help where needed. This is one reason trust is so important.

If your spouse can't get help anywhere else, they must be able to get help from their Maker and from he or she they were designed to have sex with. You and your spouse should be able to get help for your seen and unseen, spoken and unspoken needs. All of your needs, desires and curiosities should be identified and met, be satisfied, build relationship, leaving less room for the devil to move.

A CHALLENGE FOR YOU

I have another challenge for you. I want you to do everything in your power to make your body and entire essence your spouse's paradise. That's right. Sex is part of what makes marriage paradise. I dare you to become Eden for your beloved.

Become an atmosphere they can abide in safely and satisfied. Become the place where they do not need to feel ashamed about what they have or don't have, where they are free to ask questions, explore and share the desires of their heart. Let them feel and enjoy your presence. Let them enjoy your abundance.

3

SECRET PLEASURES

Thou wilt shew me the path of life: in thy presence [is] fulness of joy; at thy right hand [there are] pleasures for evermore.
Psalms 16:11

When we understand sex within the marital bounds as a pleasure that is beyond measure, we will enjoy it better. Sex should never be viewed as an arduous task. But why is it that after marriage, so many people begin to view sex as a chore or means of stress?

I believe it is because we have been provided so much false information about sex, especially those of us who grew up in church. If we have grown to believe sex is solely for the purpose of child rearing, we are going to think of sex as more of a responsibility than a God-sent pleasurable experience. Friends, it is important that we understand sex as a powerful, beautiful force of pleasure.

The Bible talks about pleasure many times, especially when it comes to how we interact with God. I call this chapter Secret Pleasures because within the marital bounds, God has hidden something especially for you. The more time you spend in intimacy with the Holy Spirit, the more He reveals things to you[7]. Likewise, the more time you spend in intimacy with your spouse, the more you find there is to enjoy.

---

[7] Psalm 16:11

SECRETS

The Bible talks about secrets often. Mysteries and secrets are a part of how Jesus partners with us to establish His kingdom on earth[8]. Secrets let you know that there is something very special, valuable and exclusive available for those who are in a relationship with the secret holder.

Secrets can come in the form of information, experiences, opportunities or tangibles. No matter how secrets are embodied, they are always exclusive and set apart to be kept between the secret holders. Sharing secrets thickens the bond between two bodies.

Secrets are the safety and preservation of valuable things and information. In this case, I suggest to you that in the marriage bed there should be something invaluable and exclusive that no one else knows about except the one

---

[8] Matthew 13:11

worthy of sharing that secret with you. The secret I am sharing with you is the secret of pleasure.

GOOD PLEASURE

Let's play a game of word association. I took a quick poll asking a few people in different phases of their life the following question: When you hear the word "pleasure" what is the very first image that comes into your mind?

Some people answered, "Sex! Good sex... the orgasm producing kind," and rightfully so! Another thought of their favorite delectable, the kind that takes them to their happy place and puts a smile on their face the moment they bite into it. Someone else imagined a luxurious hotel room or spa that was fragrant and saturated in silence and complimented with peace and perhaps a good masseuse. Still, another person heard the word, pleasure and immediately pictured one of the servers dressed in red at

Chick-fil-A bringing her meal as they touted, "It's a pleasure to serve you today!"

In all the cases, you can see a slight smile on the person's face when they thought about what pleasure looked like for them. In fact, in each scenario, it was less what pleasure looked like, and more what pleasure felt like to them.

What if I told you that good pleasure is not about what you can do that will make you feel good right now? What if I told you that pleasure had little to do with instant self-gratification?

Pleasure, at its core and origin is a verb. Its Latin root is "to please". This suggests that pleasure has more to do with your actions towards someone than it does your feelings towards something. Much like sex, the fundamental meaning and purpose of pleasure has been distorted and reduced to more of a generic term, with fundamental components missing.

For starters, one of the mysteries of pleasure is that it is designed to be experienced by both the recipient and the initiator. Let's take a look at some scriptures.

for it is God who works in you both to will and to do of His good pleasure.
Philippians 2:13

Let them shout for joy and be glad, who favor my righteous cause; and let them say continually, "Let the Lord be magnified, who has pleasure in the prosperity of His servant."
Psalm 35:27

For the Lord takes pleasure in His people; He will beautify the humble with salvation.
Psalm 149:4

Do not fear, little flock, for it is your Father's good pleasure to give you the kingdom.
Luke 12:32

Do you see a pattern here? In each of these verses the giver of pleasure takes delight and experiences his pleasure by serving the recipient.

PLEASURE: THE ANTITHESIS OF LONELINESS

Take a look at this text from scripture:

If you turn away your foot from the Sabbath, from doing your pleasure on My holy day, and call the Sabbath a delight, the holy day of the Lord, honorable, and shall honor Him, <u>not doing your own ways, nor finding your own pleasure</u>, nor speaking your own words, then you shall delight yourself in the Lord; and I will cause you to ride on the high hills of the earth and feed you with the heritage of Jacob your father. The mouth of the Lord has spoken.
Isaiah 58:13-14 (emphasis mine)

Here, the children of Israel are cautioned against self-pleasuring. Is it wrong to please yourself? Not necessarily. Is it optimal? Based on this scripture, it is not. You will enjoy pleasure when you are being pleasured and when you are giving it.

If you have ever wondered what the problem with masturbation is, this is it. Perhaps it is true you are not hurting anyone. Perhaps it is true that it feels good, but the truth is you are helping the devil do his work of keeping you in isolation. You are also not getting the real deal. You are deceiving yourself into settling for the alternative to ultimate pleasure.

Self-pleasure is out of order. It is not part of God's divine plan and it leaves room for the devil to play around in the lives of God's children. It is unreal. It is not authentic.

Adam had the capacity to express love from the moment he was created. Adam certainly was not the only creature on earth. Still, God said, it is not good that he be alone. This tells us that loneliness was never a part of God's plan. We were created for companionship.

God finds expression through His church- that is us, the man He created. Likewise, we must find our expression through our spouse, sexually and otherwise. When the Bible says, "Love your neighbor as yourself,' it implies that you must know how to love yourself. Remember, you and your spouse are one. You mustn't hold anything back when it comes to sacrificing just as God does not hold back anything when it comes to Him expressing His love to you.

THE SCIENCE OF PLEASURE

I want to buttress the point that pleasure was created as a part of God's divine strategy for mankind. Sexual pleasure has scientifically proven physical health benefits for husbands and wives. Ask your biology or medical friends and they will tell you. Everything from reduced risks of prostate cancer to improved immune systems have been found to be the resultant effect of frequent orgasms and climaxes[9].

Ladies, guess what? Studies have shown that frequent sex can regulate your menstruation and help reduce accompanying pains over time[9]. Neuroscientists have

---

[9]https://www.webmd.com/sex-relationships/guide/sex-and-health#1

studied brain activity during high pleasure experiences. The increase in blood flow and dopamine levels lead to fewer sick days, higher libido, better sleep and improved moods and energy.[10] God knew what He was doing when He created sex as a pleasurable experience.

I encourage you to do your own research as well. Maybe you can share that information with your spouse the next time they are "not feeling fine". Tell them, "Trust me, this will help you feel better."

PAY ATTENTION

Another privilege of the pleasure aspect of sex is that it teaches you to pay attention. Pleasure heavily involves your senses for a purpose. It makes it easier to pay attention to your lover's body, habits, needs and desires.

---

[10] https://www.ncbi.nlm.nih.gov/pmc/articles/PMC3008658/

Take note of your spouse's breathing patterns. Know what makes them smile. Know what brings them to orgasm. These things are important because it brings changes to your spouse's behavior or well-being to your attention in time.

Habitually pleasuring your spouse also tells them how much they really mean to you. They pay attention to the time and detail you put into pleasuring them. Imagine how much it means for you to know that God cares even about the number of hairs on your head. Now imagine what it will mean for your spouse to know that you love them enough to know when their heartbeat is pumping faster or slower than usual.

Sex, when used for its original purpose is a pure and sacred expression of covenant meant to be shared between a husband and his wedded wife. Sex is divinely designed to benefit those who legally partake in it as well as the body of Christ at large.

There is a blessing in ministry. It is not every ministry that is done from the pulpit. Ministry is ordained service- it is a righteous work you are called to do that is made holy by God. Your bedroom ministry is a powerful one. When you say, "I do" you are officially accepting the call to be a minister to your spouse and one of the ministries you have to them is the ministry of pleasure. You will gain a better and more pleasurable experience when you selflessly will to please your partner just as when you aim to please God.

4

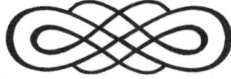

SECRET
TREASURES

For where your treasure is, there your heart will be also.
Matthew 6:21

The Bible says that the body of the believer is the temple of God where the Holy Spirit is pleased to dwell (1 Corinthians 6:19). The body as a temple. Temples are a place for sacred treasures. Such treasure is only found and enjoyed in covenant with the one who shared it.

A secret is something special and sacred and not for everyone to know and here is why: God gives us the secrets of His kingdom in hidden treasures. One of those treasures is hidden in marriage, encoded in marital sex- intimacy. One of the perks of intimacy is that it provides us with a divine means of communication that is difficult for any outsider to infiltrate. The gifts of salvation, a sense of covering and joining to form one flesh all take place for our gain and are made accessible through marital sex.

YOUR BODY IS A TEMPLE

Paul tells us, "You cannot be God's temple and continue to join your temple to a harlot". He said there's no agreement between the temple of God and Baal, an idol. There are treasures that you and your spouse are designed to carry for one another. These treasures are from God. But if your body is not maintained as a temple, there will be no room for the glorious treasures you were designed to carry.

You cannot join your temple to a harlot because it belongs to God. Likewise, you may join your temple to your wedded spouse.

The body, as a temple, communicates deeper truth about the body and sexual relations. It is two temples becoming as one. In the temple, there are great treasures. The Bible tells us in 2 Chronicles 28 that Ahaz, king of Judah, did what was evil in God's sight by opening up the temple of God and taking away articles of silver and gold to seek alignment and the pleasure of another king, a pagan king at that. The next thing that happened was that the temple was violated, and all the treasures were taken away.

Just as God commanded us to not open our temple to a harlot, He wants us to open our temple to our spouses. When your temple opens up in sexual intimacy in your marriage, you allow your spouse access to your most sacred treasures.

Treasures are meant to be treasured. Like a treasure, keep your body from casual access to everyone else except your spouse. The treasures of the temple is reserved for trusted, initiated ones. In marriage, intimacy is a treasure that must be kept within the marriage bond. It is a treasure that must be held in honor.

Your marriage is your treasure. Let it be honorable and the marriage bed undefiled (Hebrews 13:5). Marital sex is the moment where you and your beloved exchange virtues and treasures with each other: treasures of their inner most temple or of the most holy places of their being.

Your affection, your passion, your biological substances, time, breath, pain or pleasure and love are shared in this moment of intimacy. The sacrifices, commitment, honor, adoration and admiration are poured out into your spouse before, during and at the climax of intercourse. As you deposit these treasures in your spouse, your heart naturally finds a home in them and theirs in yours. Where your treasure is, there your heart will be also.

THE TREASURE OF TIME

Good sexual intimacy requires quality time in order to yield a quality experience. While there may be room occasionally for drive-by sex time, there's definitely a need for time well spent together. Create sufficient time for intimacy. This includes adequate time for foreplay and enough time to switch to new positions and to communicate with your spouse during intercourse.

Create enough time to fall into each other's arms and say, "Thank you, that was good! I enjoyed every bit of it." Those comments take time to deliver. The investment of gratitude, appreciation, love, passion and affection are treasures stored up!

"Do not cast your costly pearls **before** swine", Jesus warned in Matthew 7:6. Your treasure is not for just anyone. There is a level of attention, affection and time that only your wife or husband deserves. Not even your children deserve the amount of time your spouse does. Your children need these investments in your spouse so they can have a healthy home to grow in.

> *Again, the kingdom of heaven is like treasure hidden in a field, which a man found and hid; and for joy over it he goes and sells all that he has and buys that field.*
> **Matthew 13:44**

Remember the story of Hezekiah. He opened up his treasure for all to see.

> *...And Hezekiah was attentive to them and showed them all the house of his treasures—the silver and gold, the spices and precious ointment, and all his armory—all that was found among his treasures. There was nothing in his house or in all his dominion that Hezekiah did not show them. Then Isaiah the prophet went to King Hezekiah, and said to him, "What did these men say, and from where did they come to you?" So, Hezekiah said, "They came from a far country, from Babylon." And he said, "What have they seen in your house?" So, Hezekiah answered, "They have seen all that is in my house; there is nothing among my treasures that I have not shown them." Then Isaiah said to Hezekiah, "Hear the word of the Lord: 'Behold, the days are coming when all that is in your house, and what your fathers have accumulated until this day, shall be carried to Babylon; nothing shall be left,' says the Lord. 'And they shall take away some of your sons who will descend from you, whom you will beget; and they shall be eunuchs in the palace of the king of Babylon.'*
> **2 Kings 20: 13-18**

It did not take time for them to steal everything he had, damaging his opportunity to bring forth a legacy of kings. Don't relegate the power of pleasure that God has given you with your spouse. Cherish it as sacred and keep it holy so that you can continue to enjoy it and reap its benefits until Christ returns.

5

SEXPECTATION

I eagerly expect and hope that I will in no way be ashamed but will have sufficient courage so that now as always Christ will be exalted in my body...
Philippians 1:20

One of the most critical aspects of intimacy in a relationship is expectation. When you are expectant, you signal that you know something valuable is on the way. You testify that what is coming is worth waiting for.

For many couples, their expectations of marital sex are shaped by preconceived beliefs and misconceptions. There's the extreme of over spiritualizing sex. It is so sacred you can't even talk about it. Some couples can't even mention the word 'sex' between themselves, talk less of talking to someone else about it.

Yet, it might be the most important factor in their recurring crisis and misunderstanding and the marriage's silent killer. Someone is missing the needed satisfaction, intimacy and release that one can only get through sex with their spouse and their spouse feels their partner isn't helping them as they ought, but sex is too holy- in fact so holy they can't even talk about it. So, they fight and argue over what should be non-issues because there's a silent killer involved.

NO PRESSURE

There's the other extreme of unrealistic expectations of sex from expectations set by pornographic performances. This is where those who remained virgins and had limited to no practical sexual experiences before their current marriage are at an advantage. There's no unhealthy comparison that pushes the partner beyond limits.

The dramatic response from the partner during sexual relations such as loud moans, vibrating orgasms, oversized penis, oral sex, and sex positions do not get in the way of genuine intimacy and customized sexual pleasure that specifically meets the needs of you and your spouse with no outside influence.

The danger of expectations that come from outside experiences including pornography is that they are not for everyone. Individual responses to sex are different and porn artists are just that, artists, who are paid to act in certain ways that are not natural to everyone. The pressure of performance shouldn't be the experience for anyone in marriage. There must be growth and personal exploration of each other's bodies, pleasure spots, satisfying and comfortable positions. Exploring and discovering is the rule of the game. So, it is important to relax and create time to discover your pleasure points and your partner's.

COMMUNICATING YOUR EXPECTATIONS

Communicate your pleasure spots. Relax and allow your partner to explore your body as you give yourselves to each other in loving discoveries. This communicates trust. It is even more beautiful when you don't discover all there is to discover in a few sessions of sex of all the sex sessions of the lifetime of your marriage. The more you discover, the more you love and grow closer to your spouse.

This is where it is important to let couples know that it is okay to develop new ways you want to be touched even after 25 years into your marriage. It doesn't make you ungodly. Communicate it freely and enjoy it.

Marriage is a highly safe zone for sexual explorations. Jesus forbids lusting in your heart for another person other than your married spouse. It is adultery. This is how safe marriage makes you to be. You can desire your

own spouse. Admire and long for them. This is one way to
avoid the lust that lurks in your heart towards anyone else.
Your spouse must continue to capture your heart.

My bride, my very own, you have stolen my heart! With one
glance from your eyes and the glow of your necklace, you
have stolen my heart.
Song of Solomon 4:9 (CEV)

BE AN INITIATOR

Another expectation is about who initiates sex in the
home. Some traditions and cultures have said the woman is
to be seen, not heard. In such cultures, the woman can't say,
"I'm in the mood right now" to her husband. The woman is
not even allowed to make the first move. However, anyone
who desires sex first should express that desire and
communicate it in a way their spouse understands.

Initiating sex communicates more than just, "Hey!
it's time for sex" to your partner. It also communicates, "I
want you". Everyone wants to be wanted, not as the most

wanted in America, but to be desired. It helps to build self-esteem. Most women feed on this a lot. That sense of being desired especially despite the changing body structures. To be desired is something that feeds their sense of worth. But don't think that men do not feed on that too. Yes, they do. They may have faced some rejection or sense of loss of value and worth due to business failures, or financial issues, but to be desired by your woman after all that, is most reassuring and boosts self- esteem.

So, when you think about who initiates sex first, think about who gives that esteem first and who does it most, that's the person who is serving their partner the best. This is how to lift off the pressure about feeling cheap or feeling unserious because you're needing sex in your own marriage.

Saying no to advances can be damaging because you're not saying no to sex, you're saying more than that or rather your partner is getting more than a no to sex for now, they may be getting "I don't want you" kind of message which you innocently do not intend to send.

There are better ways of communicating tiredness or a "not now" response to sex initiation. "Sorry Honey, not right now," with a kiss, hug, cuddle or a promise of the best sex in the morning or by weekend works well. A "quickie notice" is also something to think about depending on why you're not in the mood. "Babe, I can't go all the way this time. Can we do a quickie?" You may also code it.

CREATIVE DISCRETION

Not everything is for everyone to know. Everything sex-related is to be enjoyed intimately between you and your spouse. Be mindful of who can see or hear your sexual interactions, no matter how innocent or wholesome the intention. You do not want to leave room for anyone or anything else to enter your marital union. I cannot stress enough that it is for you, your spouse and God, alone.

Mind your surroundings. Your bedroom may have very thin walls and not be sound proofed enough to avoid neighbors or children hearing what should only be between the two of you. Another reason is that you do not want to say what might kill the excitement. Be sensitive to your spouse's physical and emotional needs and feelings. "Are you almost done?" and "I really got to go now," can kill excitement. But saying, "I love you," to bring him or her to climax won't.

Saying, "Go harder," might sound too unholy, but "7up" doesn't. Let's say your husband is busy talking on the phone or to a visitor and the wife is ready. "Honey, do we have an appointment?" sounds far more innocent to guests than, "Bae, are we having sex tonight because I'm in the mood and I don't want to sleep off before you come to the room."

You can say something like, "Number 1 is so excited right now" to your wife at the park or on the bus or in the car with others. All of these have to do with being tuned in... being attuned... being one flesh in order to become more sensitive to one another and sensing the needs of your spouse and meeting them accurately.

There are many things you can do to communicate your sexual needs to your spouse in a manner that is creatively discrete. That the kids are around does not mean you can't stylishly tell your partner what you need. Let me share a few easy ways to talk about sex explicitly without being so explicit.

Give your sex parts a name. Apples, Cherries, Freeman, Number 1 are all examples of clever names you can refer to when you want your partner to give them a rub, suck or touch. You can do the same for your sexual activities. Remember the story of Hezekiah. These names and codes should be kept secret between you and your spouse- these should be names and codes only you two know.

124 can be breast caressing, 2D can be your signal to bite both nipples. When a woman wants the man to increase thrusts harder...7up. When the man is about to ejaculate... I'm on 10. When the woman is ready for him to ejaculate...I love you.

6

FANTASY

*Let the words of my mouth, and the meditation of my heart,
be acceptable in thy sight, O Lord, my strength, and my
redeemer.*
Philippians 4:8 KJV

Fantasy can be a world of endless imaginations- A journey with no end. As believers, we must be careful with sexual fantasies. Married people don't need to dwell in the world of fantasies when they can have what they could be thinking about. This is why adequate sexual satisfaction within the home is highly important. The mind is to be dedicated to the meditation of the Word of God and the pure love of others in our hearts.

Most fantasies are developed from porn addiction or exposures and other materials like novels and movies that continue to paint endless sexual adventures in the mind. This is why believers must control what they watch, see, read and entertain. An unsatisfied sexual desire can be driven about endlessly in the world of sexual fantasies. But a satisfied one will become more fruitful more frequently in other matters of life and destiny.

There are people who get disconnected from their real spouse even when they have sex with them, they allow their minds to wonder away because what's in front of them doesn't excite their appetite anymore. Partners help each other to stay in shape, stay sexy, stay physically and sexually appealing, explore certain adventures that are safe and clean, such as wearing certain intimate wears for each other as desired and communicated between them. The idea is when you bring it home, it reduces the need for the mind to wander around for it.

Honest communication of unwanted fantasies that pop-up occasionally based on past movies, books or experiences will help the partner. They should not repress it and hope it goes away. It may lead to sexual frustration. It should be communicated, naked and unashamed. Then steps should be taken to safely replace fantasies with enjoyable and achievable realities within the marriage bond that makes the fantasy go away or achieved in reality of marital sexual interactions.

Surfing lustfully through internet pornography and sexualized social media accounts, playing with sex toys, sexting and flirting over chats and texts do the same wreckage that adultery and fornication do to your soul. Flee every appearance of evil. Do not give the devil a foothold in your heart and wonder why he is not leaving your children and family alone.

Therefore, Jesus' law about looking lustfully at a woman that makes it as though a man has already committed adultery in his heart gives us an understanding of virtual sex here. So, if you connect sexually with your partners in your heart even when you are not physically able to due to fatigue and other things, you are still connected sexually.

This is where romantic communications and flirting with your own spouse will help you stay connected sexually and relax. This also signals the danger of virtual sex situations with anything or anyone other than your own spouse.

WHOLESOMENESS

The boundaries for sexual activities within the marriage bond must be set by the desires of both partners according to what is wholesome. Wholesome will be defined by how it helps to satisfy the need of the partner. How it helps to prevent unnecessary longing and lusts. How it helps to achieve emotional connection between the couple. The bond that seals the union so much that it prevents external interests, attractions or interferences in the level of sexual intimacy and communication.

FANTASIES CAN BE WILD

Fantasy could include how to get away with a spouse to a hotel for one night away from home or roses and candles. You can imagine having sex with your spouse in the kitchen, living room or in the stairways when no one else is around. Blindfolds and handcuffs are harmless if it is desirable, fun and consensual for you both.

Such things don't suggest anything negative. Imagining your spouse in a particular dress or outfit, harmless. If the goal of the fantasy is satisfying your partner and is desirable to each of you, enjoy your fantasy. The risk of fantasies is that you can also go too far. Be sensitive enough to strike a balance and stay within the marital bonds.

Sexual intimacy is a form of communication. It is a place of intimate exchange. When you start to add things from the outside to this intimate form of communication, it begins to damage the frequency. You also risk transmitting harmful things to your spouse.

Fantasies are appropriate when they move you to act in a way that is productive and fruitful. When they do the opposite, beware. The risk of fantasizing about things outside of your marriage is that it ignites a blaze of separation, just like sin does. Images of others, inflicting pain on another are examples of bringing outside entities into your intimate communication.

The Apostle Paul gives us this counsel that was inspired by God Himself to guide our thought flow and to keep us pure in heart.

Finally, brethren, whatsoever things are true, whatsoever things are honest, whatsoever things are just, whatsoever things are pure, whatsoever things are lovely, whatsoever things are of good report; if there be any virtue, and if there be any praise, think on these things.
Philippians 4:8

May this word guide you and keep you and your marriage safe in Jesus' mighty name.

7

CLOSER +DEEPER

As the deer pants for the water brooks, so pants my soul for You, O God.
Psalm 42:1

Just as you should desire a deeper, closer walk with God daily, you should desire to be closer to your spouse. You should guard yourself against anything that gets in the way of this desire for closeness, including the sexual challenges that might arise.

But let's be clear. Sex is made for marriage, not the other way around. Everything we do in marriage mustn't be for the sake of sex alone. Every sexual act, thought and word exchanged must be for the strengthening of the marriage.

Don't relegate the power and pleasure that sex makes available to married believers by not treating sex like a vital activity for a healthy, productive, Christ-centered marriage.

THINGS WE MUST RESOLVE

There are conditions and experiences that people have endured that impact sexual health. Such experiences and conditions can make it difficult for people to fully enjoy the power and pleasure of intercourse with their spouse. Child abuse, molestation, rape, certain medical conditions and the like can heavily impact a person's ability to be intimate with their spouse.

If you have experienced or are currently experiencing any of the aforementioned and their associated effects, do not ignore or dismiss the problem. In fact, be sure you see it as a problem and not something you just have to accept. Work to find a solution to these issues and challenges with the help of God, your spouse and a professional as applicable.

Everything that impacts your capacity to be intimate must be dealt with. The devil loves to do whatever he can to keep the children of God suffering and in isolation. If he can help it, he will desire that you become comfortable in disease and in anything that keeps you separate from the body of Christ, your spouse and most importantly from God Himself.

Recognize things that limit your capacity to truly love and live the life that God has called you to. If you choose not to do anything about it, you are choosing not to get the best out of marriage, or the best God has for you in life. You are also choosing to cheat your husband or wife. Remember, the two of you are called to be one. Whatever harms you harms them, too. God has called you to a life of healing and wholeness. To settle for less is dangerous for you and it is also cheating those people He put into your life to be blessed by your very existence, especially your spouse.

Your salvation experience can do away with many of the struggles and the residual consequences of past experiences and sicknesses that you were susceptible to prior to your decision to follow Christ. But there are some things you will need to address directly both in the natural and in the spiritual, if possible, prior to marriage. If it is not possible to address before marriage because it is too late or you are just now identifying the problem, then you must take the necessary steps to work through these challenges, preferably not alone.

First, let's talk about the things that marriage and marital sex can cure with time. Let me share a scriptural passage with you about King David who was coming of age and experiencing some sickness in his body.

Now king David was old and stricken in years; and they covered him with clothes, but he got no heat. Wherefore his servants said unto him, let there be sought for my lord the king a young virgin: and let her stand before the king, and let her cherish him, and let her lie in thy bosom, that my lord the king may get heat. So they sought for a fair damsel throughout all the coasts of Israel, and found Abishag a Shunammite, and brought her to the king. And the damsel

*was very fair, and cherished the king, and ministered to
him: but the king knew her not.*
1 Kings 1:1-4 KJV

There is power in physical touch. Do you see how closeness and attention alone was enough to comfort David? In situations where sex is not possible, you can minister to your spouse just by being attentive to their issue, laying with them and caressing them. Sexual intimacy is about more than physical penetration. It can and should include the penetration of the heart and mind. Such can be healing.

It is important that as a husband or wife, you take up this role for your spouse especially when penetration is not an option. Remember, I told you that there are some things that prevent us from being close to others, especially to our spouse. The devil wants it that way so that we can never experience the power of true intimacy. Rather he wants to pacify us with a false sense of pleasure through channels such as pornography, masturbation, perverse fantasies or even the taking on of false senses of identity or preferences such as homosexuality and transgendered identities.

Don't leave room for you or your spouse's minds to wander. Use physical touch, caress, whispering romantic declarations of love and admiration and every sensual thing within the bounds of the marital covenant to keep the fire of intimacy between the two of you ever burning. Lost for ideas, do not worry, I am going to share some very explicit ones with you soon and prayerfully these will help you to ignite the passion and fire your marriage deserves.

SPIRITUAL

There are some wounds only Jesus can heal. In fact, He should be your first resort any time sickness arises in your body. This goes for spiritual, mental and physical sickness. As children of God, you have God-given tools to make your healing a reality through Christ Jesus. The bible says in Matthew 10:8:

*Heal the sick, cleanse the lepers, raise the dead, cast out
demons. Freely you have received, freely give.*
Matthew 10:8

So, if you and your spouse are believers, you have
divinely distributed grace and authority to cast out any
sickness and disease you are facing and declare healing over
your lives. You can lay hands on your spouse and vice versa
with confident expectation that healing is sure. This is a
standard grace for everyone who follows Christ.

If there is anything in you that seems dead or that is
not functioning at the standard God designed it to function
originally, the word of God says this:

*But if the Spirit of Him who raised Jesus from the dead
dwells in you, He who raised Christ from the dead will also
give life to your mortal bodies through His Spirit who
dwells in you.*
Romans 8:11

It is all about your faith confession. You have a
right to declare on you and your spouse everything God has
declared in His word concerning you. Tell your spouse, by

His stripes, she is healed. Tell your man that you decree and declare life and healing to his body, mind and spirit.

There are some instances where you might need help. Don't be afraid to ask for it. The bible says in the book of James:

Is anyone among you sick? Let him call for the elders of the church, and let them pray over him, anointing him with oil in the name of the Lord. And the prayer of faith will save the sick, and the Lord will raise him up. And if he has committed sins, he will be forgiven.
James 5:14-15

How do you know when you need to "call for the elders"? Any time what you are dealing with seems more than you can bear, when you are in the place of crisis, and when you simply do not know what to do, you do not need to hesitate to make an appointment to consult your pastor or trusted men and women of your life. They can pray over you and counsel you and encourage your faith. They can even give you practical counsel to follow.

NATURAL

There are some issues that God has already placed solutions to in the hands of men including medical doctors, medicine and therapists. Jesus had professionals in his ministry crew. Do not be afraid or too deep to see a medical professional if the need arises. It takes faith for medications and the rest to work for you. Husbands, see your local urologist. Wives, see your gynecologist. See your primary care doctors. You can pray for the right one to see but please follow through with your routine medical examinations and seek medical attention for medical problems. If you know what God has said concerning you and if you are praying, there is nothing the doctor can tell you that God cannot fix or that He has not given you a solution for.

One advise I would give is that you take precaution when adding anything to your bodies. Know side effects and purpose and be sure you really need what is being prescribed to you. Do not take medications frivolously. Take them as needed and according to doctors' orders. Do not take every herb your friend recommends. Talk to professionals and get counsel from trusted Christian professionals as much as possible.

Take care of yourselves. Eat healthy. Learn what foods you must avoid. Drink plenty of water and get rest. Exercise. Avoid stress by living a balanced life. Help one another do the same. Try not to stress each other out. Help each other with your weight management goals as applicable. All these things impact your sexual health and your spirit man as well. Remember that your body is the temple of God and that it also belongs to your spouse. Treat your bodies with care. Treat each other with care, physically, mentally and of course spiritually. Find what works for you both and be consistent. Check in with each other to be sure you are maintaining a balance in life that includes routine, wholistic (physical, spiritual, mental) care.

The other major natural solution is not running away from what is not comfortable because of past experiences. Be honest with your spouse and be understanding with one another. Take it slow, but try. Try more foreplay, slowly. Check in with each other about how it feels and find out what your spouse might need from you to make it work. Remember, your bodies are for each other. You should be able to touch and know every part of one another. Explore each other and pleasure every part of each other. Do not shy away from using your hands, lips, tongue, hands, mouth and especially your hearts to nurture intimacy between you and your lover. You belong to each other and both of you belong to God who has graciously given you to one another.

MIND RENEWAL

I once watched a documentary that told the story of some women who go through excruciating pains during sex. The documentary focused more on the cause being their religious background that made them associate pains with sex in their minds until their bodies started to resist the experience of sex as a pleasurable one.

Your mind is powerful, and it is a battlefield. Your mind can determine the kinds of experiences you have in life. It impacts your perception and your beliefs.

Especially if you have had traumatic experiences related to sex, and also if you have learned maladaptive attitudes or sexual behaviors, it is critical that with your salvation and deliverance experience that you renew your mind regularly. This is a standard Christian practice anyway, but you must be more sensitive to making it a priority as it pertains to your ability to have a healthy sex life.

How do you renew your mind? Think about what God has said concerning issues. Meditate on His promises that have been written down in His word just for you. The bible says,

> *Let this mind be in you which was also in Christ Jesus, who, being in the form of God, did not consider it robbery to be equal with God, but made Himself of no reputation, taking the form of a bondservant, and coming in*

the likeness of men. And being found in appearance as a man, He humbled Himself and became obedient to the point of death, even the death of the cross. Therefore, God also has highly exalted Him and given Him the name, which is above every name, that at the name of Jesus every knee should bow, of those in heaven, and of those on earth, and of those under the earth, and that every tongue should confess that Jesus Christ is Lord, to the glory of God the Father.
Philippians 2:5-11

And do not be conformed to this world, but be transformed by the renewing of your mind, that you may prove what is that good and acceptable and perfect will of God.
Romans 12:2

Don't allow your thoughts to hold you captive. Take charge of them, replacing every negative or counterproductive thought with God's word.

MAKE IT A PRIORITY

As a married couple, you must make sexual intimacy a priority. You might be wondering, "How can we have regular sexual connection with our busy life?" The problem with the frequency of sex in marriages has to do with stress on at least one of the partners due to work and children and other family or financial situations.

Some of those are normal situations that should not kill the sexual passion in your relationship. You simply need to create time for it. If you understand how beneficial regular sex is in light of busy and complex schedules, you will make room for it.

No one has ever been too busy to eat though they are busy. So why starve your marriage its food because you're busy. Yes, maybe sometimes you forgot to eat because of busy schedules, but you sure got something to eat to keep body and soul together. I have heard some women ask, "Is sex food?" The answer is yes, it is food for your marriage.

Treat sex like that and you'll see why you make room for it no matter what you're going through. Even in sickness, when you lost appetite, it's still dangerous for you to try going on without food for long period of time. You'll need that food to recuperate. Sex is food for your marriage.

YIELDING

The willingness to yield is a powerful force that unites the two involved. By that, I mean that you do not have to have sex to be connected to your spouse, your willingness to have sex even though you are physically unable to will go a long way to achieve the same connection of the soul that is necessary to keep the union and oneness going.

You can connect in your mind sexually with the one you are married to when you cannot do it physically.

Therefore, Jesus' law about looking lustfully at a woman that makes it as though a man has already committed adultery in his heart gives us an understanding of virtual sex here.

So, if you connect sexually with your partner in your heart even when you are not physically able to due to fatigue and other things, you are still connected sexually. This is where romantic communications and flirting with your own spouse will help you stay connected sexually and relax. This also signals the danger of virtual sex situations with anything or anyone other than your own spouse.

CLOSER

Sex separates the husband and wife from any other relationships on the earth. Healthy sexual encounters build a wall of protection around the married couple that sets them apart from everyone else. When you are intimately involved with someone sexually, you are sharing a part of your life with them that you never will share with anyone else in life ever. So, not only does it unite you together, but it also separates your marriage from all other kinds of relationships. It sets your relationship apart as a unique union.

Remember, sex consecrates you to your wedded spouse. It establishes the fact that you belong to each other like no other. This separation helps to give the union a unique identity and purpose on the earth. Imagine that it is the only thing you do with your wife or husband that you will never do with any other person forever!

It is like your individual fingerprint that has no match anywhere else in the world. It builds a wall of protection and defense around you and not allow you to be open to attacks like a city without walls. In sex, your innermost being is open for the innermost treasure of your partner so you can deposit life into each other.

SEX IS A GATEWAY

Sex is the gateway to the soul. If through the sexual union, oneness is achieved even with a harlot, the Bible says, there is something in that union that opens the partners up in their innermost part to receive and to give their deepest treasures that makes them part of each other and unites them.

The point of the intense pleasure or pain is an opener of the soul. People give up the ghost with either intense pain or pleasure depending on the status of their soul and their physical condition when they go. In the same way, the spirit is shared at the point of intense pleasure. There is sharing of the spirit that must happen between you and your spouse.

There are religions that make use of sexual encounters to do rituals and worship. Why? They know that it is a way of opening to the covering spirits. In the same way, your sex moments can be moments of worship, sacred between the two of you and allowing the Spirit of God to be Lord over your spirits and to keep you united in the oneness that empowers you two to chase your ten thousand.

8

CASE STUDIES

Study to shew thyself approved unto God, a workman that needeth not to be ashamed, rightly dividing the word of truth.
2 Timothy 2:15

To study requires more than just the acquisition of knowledge. True studying is application and putting to test all the knowledge you have acquired over time until you demonstrate mastery. When it comes to going beyond monotonous and mediocre married sex lives and journeying into unfettered intimacy, you have to put in the work!

No matter what you are struggling with in marriage, no matter what may ail or haunt you, by now, you and your spouse have the information you need to conquer it to enjoy a robust, pleasure-filled and life-giving sex life.

We have covered many things. It is time to put our new knowledge to the test to show ourselves approved. Maybe you and your spouse can make a game out of these. Read each case study carefully as if you are a marriage counselor. Whichever spouse gets it right can choose the intimate activity you two can engage in next. Have fun!

CASE STUDY ONE

Imagine you are a Christian marriage counselor. A husband shares the pains of living with his good wife whom he is madly in love with and aroused by. Due to circumcision, she does not enjoy sex at all. He gets frustrated every time she seems to reject, dismiss or ignore sexual advances. Their marriage is on the verge of collapse. What can they do to restore the marriage?

CASE STUDY TWO

Imagine you are a Christian marriage counselor. A young pastor and his wife come to you looking completely distressed. "I can't cope with this anymore!" the young pastor and husband announces. You ask what the problem is and the wife replies, "My husband wants to separate! You just want to give up and you call yourself a pastor!" She begins to cry.

Her husband responds, "It's you that wants the separation. I love you. I pour out almost every Sunday and all during the week and you can't give me anything without making me feel like an inconvenience. You think you are too good to have sex with me? Or I am too much for you? You make me feel like I am being violent or barbaric for wanting sex with my wife! You act like you are in complete pain and disgust every time I try to reach out to you romantically. You push me away and I am tired of it. In fact, I need to take a walk. I am leaving. I will be back" and just like that, the young pastor storms out of the office.

When he leaves, his wife discloses to you that she found out she has cysts that cause her pain with every sexual encounter. She is afraid to tell her husband because she does not know what the cysts mean and does not want to him to fear. What should they do?

CASE STUDY THREE

Another couple comes in and the wife shares with you her painful experiences during sex. Her husband complains about her not being naturally lubricated. You then find out that she was circumcised. They seem to lack knowledge about how to be lubricated or enjoy sex generally. What do you tell them?

CASE STUDY FOUR

"My husband is just too crazy! He likes to just have sex out of the blue! One time he tried to surprise me with a blindfold… I wore the blind fold thinking he bought me a new car and when I took it off, he was standing there naked wearing a bow and dancing for me! What do I do?" Her husband quickly interjected, "She too is crazy. She requires the most extreme cases just to be in the mood. She wants every day to be like Valentine's Day. I have to feed her strawberries, buy her flowers and set candles just for a kiss. It is all too much! What do I do?" Well, what do you think they should do?

CASE STUDY FIVE

About a month ago, a couple gave birth to their sixth child, each child is just a year apart. On top of this, both husband and wife run their own businesses and the businesses are growing very quickly. "…and we just closed on a new house too! We move in next week! We are really expanding and doing great! We love this life, but things are really getting busy! I notice my wife is seeming a little more stressed out. What do we do? Should we just wait for this season to pass before we think about intimacy… As you can see by our six children, intimacy had never been a problem in the past." What will you tell them?

CONCLUSION

But he that is married careth for the things that are of the world, how he may please his wife.
1 Corinthians 7:33

To marry requires some care for the natural things of the world or the marriage will not work. We are not of this world and definitely do not take on that mindset. But we must acknowledge that as long as we are in the world, there are natural things God has given us access to and authority over so that we can enjoy the best of life on this side of eternity.

To please God, you must be able to please your partner. Scripture tells us that we cannot say we love God, and we have neighbors we struggle to show love to, talk less of our spouses (1 John 4:20). Remember, pleasure is a critical part of the marriage covenant. Most Christian homes fail because of the failure to recognize this. The only way to get out of this responsibility of knowing how to adequately pleasure your spouse is to stay unmarried, which Paul leaves open as an option.

My main point is this: to please your partner is not a sin against God. It is honoring to Him. Getting married means preparing yourself to be a pleasure to your spouse. You can be doing almost everything in your power to please God, but if pleasing your spouse is not a part of what you do to let God know you appreciate who He has sent you, then you are missing a vital point of worship and your marriage may flatline as a result. A failed marriage is of no pleasure to the Most High.

Pleasing your husband or wife as a care of the world doesn't include going into any sinful practices or thought flows. God helps you that you do not marry someone who would make you go as far as sinning to please them. But the point is this, once you marry, you must prepare to please your spouse. God is pleased within the marriage context as you please your spouse.

If you chose to marry, you chose to live a life of pleasure. As you can see, the root of that word pleasure is to please. You must choose to please your spouse. You must choose to please God with all that you do in the marital union- including sex.

If you are married and you choose to leave and go do missionary work overseas for extended periods of time without thinking about or consulting your spouse or moving on one accord, there is a problem there. In the bedroom, if you choose to do sex in the way that is most convenient for you without considering the desire of your spouse, you are in the wrong. Marriage and sex are not designed to work like that.

When you operate your marriage and marital sex life outside the intention of giving pleasure to God and your spouse, you may lose your spouse to continuous burning desires they have that were never met. A wife may be lured away into infidelity or get it out in other ways that ultimately create frustration, anger and strife for the entire family.

As a loving deer and a graceful doe, let her breasts satisfy you at all times; And always be enraptured with her love.
Proverbs 5:19

Every child of God must make it their aim to glorify God in all things including in their bodies which are God's. We glorify God when we abide in Him (1 Corinthians 6:20). This includes not engaging in sexual activities that do not glorify God.

There's no reason to keep burning with desires when you're married. The bible says:

But if they cannot contain, let them marry for it is better to marry than to burn.
1 Corinthians 7:9 KJV

Your marriage should be a safe space to get your desires met within the bounds of the marital union. It is also a safe space to ensure your desires are purified. In marriage, you learn to yield, surrender and sacrifice all the things God requires of us if we want to follow Jesus effectively. In marriage, we learn to love unconditionally which should give us a deeper appreciation for the love Christ Jesus has for us.

For the unbelieving husband is sanctified by the wife, and the unbelieving wife is sanctified by the husband: else were your children unclean; but now are they holy.
1 Corinthians 7:14

This one speaks to sex as a process of sanctification. When you enter into such a covenant, something of one can come upon the other and it either sanctifies them or makes them unclean. You are called to strengthen and purify each other through your union. Pray for each other. Cover each other. Pray with each other and lay with each other. Enjoy every aspect of your marriage covenant and never stop working to enhance it. May your marriage and sexual intimacy continue growing from strength to strength and glory to glory, in Jesus' name.

ACKNOWLEDGMENT

I give thanks to God for His amazing love and grace. God, You are the greatest Lover in the Universe. Thank you for showing us how it's done, Sir.

I appreciate my wife who shares the deepest intimacy with me and remains my best friend, lover and playmate. Thank you for being vulnerable with me for these many years and for inspiring me to share from our secret place.

To the 7th Seal Advantage, Sherilynn who edited and made this book a good read for everyone. Thank you for your sleepless nights and for your sacrifice and skills.

To all those who have shared their bedroom experiences with me in confidence, thank you for your trust and for allowing others to rise through what seemed to be your fall. What the enemy meant for evil, is turned for good.

To my fountain of inspiration, my precious friend and senior partner, The Holy Spirit. Thank you for your sweet fellowship and your ever flowing oil upon my head and my pen.

www.ingramcontent.com/pod-product-compliance
Lightning Source LLC
Chambersburg PA
CBHW070817050426
42452CB00011B/2080